I0459693

POINT BLANK

ONE

The Blatant Truth about Relationships

Troy E. Williams

ISBN: 978-1-966615-08-8 (Paperback)
ISBN: 978-1-966615-09-5 (Ebook)

CONTENTS

I want to thank the Lord God for blessing me with the ability to write. And my dad, Ronald Williams, for pushing that ability.

INTRODUCTION

The reason that has inspired me to write this book is the almost certain demise of relationships as they exist today. I've often pondered how two people could come together, becoming the love of each other's world at that time, and they can't think about anything else except this other person, morning and night. They eat, sleep, and drink this other person, acting as though they cannot even exist without their very being. The fluttering of their hearts every time they meet, the tingling excitement for the anticipation of a phone call or a visit, blind to everything else that exist around them.

Suddenly, in a matter of months (a few years if you're lucky), that same passion and love that you could not once live without can somehow transform into the most unimaginable hatred two people could ever experience. Now all of a sudden, the same person who you thought you could no way live without turns your stomach at every sight. Every action he or she used to do now seems to rub you the wrong way; every conversation that comes from your mouth seems to create an argument. All the things that you had in common have now turned out to be all the things that irk you the most. The pet names you used to have for each other have now turned to vicious name-calling, bordering on verbal abuse. Public outbursts become a common occurrence, sometimes even turning into physical abuse.

This intense hatred seems to just get worse the longer you stay together, sometimes leading to incarcerations, or in worst cases, even death.

How does this passion turn from love to hate in what seems to be such a short period of time? The blatant truth about relationships will reveal why relationships deteriorate so quickly.

You will surely find where you fit in one of these chapters, because we all have been there!

1

Mistaken Identities

The phrase "mistaken identity" refers to that significant other when you meet for the first time. With both men and women, this is equally dispersed.

Our mistake is that we let our emotions pass our first judgment. This clouds our perception of the little signs that we should have picked up in the beginning. Paying attention to the little signs, gestures, and spoken phrases often reveal details of a person's true personality which we could focus on. And the reason that this is so important—and the biggest mistake we make in the beginning—is because the person who you are meeting there at that moment is not the person you will know in the next few months or years.

This is the representative we use to make our introductions to one another. And this is where the first signs of trouble are seeded in the relationship.

People can only keep up facades for so long; the true you will come through sooner or later—sooner if you live together.

Crazy as this may sound, but the best approach is the direct approach. The moment you begin to feel that it may develop into some sort of relationship, personal issues should be placed on the table. But this takes much too much courage. Imagine letting someone know (who you think you're about to spend a long time with) all your issues, faults, and personal quirks. But if you do, this will allow the person to analyze the situation and then make a decision. Just think: if the significant other does decide to proceed into the relationship, the chances of it being successful and long lasting are greatly increased.

But the representative we send forth sets up standards that you have to now live up to every time you're with this person. If your hair is done, your teeth are white, your body smell is sensuous, your attire is of a sexy, attractive nature, then this is what the person you are now meeting has come to expect from you. If this is not who you really are, it is a problem waiting to happen. If you have the opportunity to talk in the first meeting, open up and be yourself. It is okay to let that person know that "Hey, I am just out having a good time. Don't think that I take the time to glam up like this every day." This will lower the other person's expectations, and when he or she sees you the next time and you're in jeans or sweats, he or she is not taken aback.

As I said before, this takes a lot of courage and self-confidence, but relationships should be considered important enough that you would want to establish the strongest foundation possible. Remember, what is concealed in the dark will always be revealed in the light.

2

From a Man to a Boy

T he title itself is almost self-explanatory. You meet the woman of your dreams, and for a while, the earth moves whenever you're together. A man's nature is to want to please a woman, make her happy, and keep a smile on her beautiful face. No matter what it is she requests, if it is within his power, he will try and deliver. And during this period, when you're able to fulfill all her needs, it seems a strange thing begins to happen. Very, very subtle at the beginning, so subtle that by the time a man becomes aware of this, he is already in too deep, changed from a man to a boy. This is not something that the female does intentionally, but she will eventually end up capitalizing on this in the near future; more often than not, it's the male's fault, too. For what is accepted in the beginning of the relationship cannot be changed later down the road.

To be absolutely honest, I'm not really sure how to avoid this inevitable occurrence. For as the relationship starts out in its infant stage, the more a man seeks to please the woman, the more the balance of power seems to shift in her favor. A lot of this probably has to do with the natural nurturing, mother instinct that is in most women, and the little boy that is in most men.

Either way, this becomes a problem and causes lots of stress on most relationships, specifically from the male's point of view. Slowly but surely, it seems the man starts to regress from the man he was before she came into his life, going from a significant other to almost becoming her child.

Why is it that a grown man who goes out and works hard every day, provides for his family, pays the bills, and protects his family ends up in a position where whenever he's not home, he feels that he has to check in constantly.

Be out late in the evening with the guys drinking, gambling, or whatever, and suddenly, your cell phone begins to ring and she will have any silly reason to be calling you. But this is her way of finding out what you're up. Yes, you can call it "courtesy to call," but the balance of power has now shifted more to her side. Most men do not usually call his woman when she is out with the girls, or shopping, or whatever it is that women like to do.

Men usually cherish this time when she is out. But why, on the other hand, when the man is out, a woman usually uses this time to let her imagination run wild?

Soon, small remarks about your clothing begin to creep in. You begin to get comments like "Are you sure you want to wear that?" or "That really doesn't match what you're wearing." Now, you seem to have been fine with the way you dressed when you first got her attention, so how did you lose your taste in the short time span you have been with her?

And your friends, the same ones you hung around with when you met her and was dating her, are no longer acceptable. And gradually, they begin to fall off. It now seems that all of your time away from home has to now be accounted for. Without even realizing it, you are on the clock from the moment you leave your house, when the exact same instance is not the same for her. How does this come to be?

Some relationships even deteriorate to the extent that when couples argue, the man is berated as though he were her child and actually being scolded for things he should or shouldn't do. The male can be constantly apologizing until he is blue in the face, but to no avail. Why does a woman subconsciously seek to transform her man to a boy? Is it for the balance of power? Is it for total control in the relationship?

The action and the question are both perplexing because deep down, most women do not want a man who doesn't have a backbone.

They look for a man who can take charge, make decisions, and protect the family. But it seems the more backbone a man seeks to establish, the more confrontation he is met with from his significant other. This, I tell you honestly, I have no answer for. But you can bet, given enough time, it will surely happen. Later, we will delve into the different kinds of men (as well as women), and then you may be able to find the answer for yourself.

3

Why He Cheats

Both sexes will find this to be one of the more interesting chapters in the book, especially from a female perspective. Women have been baffled, since the notion of relationships came into existence, on why their man would cheat.

As I elaborate on this subject, please bear in mind that the book I am writing reveals the blatant truth of relationships and that I am in no way saying I condone any of the reasons I am about to write about. As I myself have searched this mystery, I have found it odd that even in the animal kingdom, males have problems with monogamy. Even in the Bible, there was only one monogamous male throughout all history. Again, I say I am not trying to justify, just stating the facts.

Okay, enough foreplay. Let's get to the goods. Women are about to find this next part something they probably don't agree with, but the funny thing is that sometimes, it's their own fault what causes their man to cheat. Men are not all that complex. We're basically very simple creatures. If a woman dates a man for at least a year, she can basically find out what she has for the upcoming future; like saying goes, what you see is what you get. Men don't spend a lot of time in their mistaken-identity representative mode.

Usually, once the sexual act has occurred, he begins to act as he will probably be acting the entire time you're with him, for better or for worse. The woman, on the other hand, only drops her facades in layers over a period of time. So for a man, you really don't get to know who your woman really is until an allotment of time has passed in the relationship. And this time frame varies from woman to woman.

Now, back to why I say it's sometimes a woman's fault infidelity sets in to relationships. One of the major reasons should be a lot more obvious to women than they care to acknowledge. Women need to constantly reflect back to the very beginning of the relationship they are now so tired of. They need to remember that the man committed to them made that commitment more than likely to her representative she first put forth to him (i.e., mistaken identity).

Remember the girl he met, who loved to have fun, was so spontaneous, the one who was so sexually uninhibited.

Especially here in the sexual arena, you cannot begin to enter into a relationship with a man enjoying wild and uninhibited sex in strange places, doing unusual positions, and then in four or five months down the road just shut it down. You can't go from thongs and boy shorts to bloomer panties. You can't go from sexy hairstyles to nappy heads and head rags. You can't go from sexy lingerie to full-length cotton zip-up robes and footy pajamas, and then looked totally puzzled why your man is suddenly straying! Now let's be real, Ladies. If this is what you presented to him from the very beginning, do you think he would have committed to you? Honestly? And yet, you asked why he wanders off when things change to this.

My question is: where does that exciting woman go? You know she's in there somewhere. Why do females feel the need to bury that side of themselves once they solidified a relationship? You can probably count on the fact that the man is still acting pretty much the same as when you first met him, so why is it such a drastic change from the female standpoint once the relationship gets some foundation? Now, it's just too much effort to keep your hair done, you just don't feel like dressing nice (not even sexy), and those special sexual things are now reserved for birthdays and special occasions (if then). Sex itself, even some time, is treated like a chore, when she just rolls over on her side and tells you to hurry up. What the hell is that? But as I said, that's just one of the reasons men have issues with them, too. I believe the man's first and foremost problem is the mental standpoint of infidelity. I'm going to give you the basic man's reasoning, keeping in mind I'm not saying any of this is okay. I am in no way saying that a man cannot be monogamous; it's just the effort he must put forth that is in question. You see, a man's reasoning is so lopsided it's not even funny. A man will tell you there is absolutely nothing wrong with his woman or that what she is doing is causing him to cheat. It is just plain animalistic, sexual desire that tempts him to stray and the thought of variety that blinds him. It's a given fact that sex is a major part of any relationship, coupled with the fact that no two women do it alike keeps a constant temptation dangling in front of a man's face.

Sometimes, this outside sex may be coupled with the fact that the man can tell the other woman things he is not comfortable talking to his woman about. Men also have this strange way of being able to totally detach themselves from any emotional feelings derived from outside sex, which makes us concoct this insane notion that as long as we are not creating a relationship or bringing any children into the world, we are not taking anything from our primary relationship. We are still good providers, protectors, and supporters to our families. And we usually don't feel guilty because we figure our partners know our needs, and that they wouldn't find out— unless, of course, they are caught!

Personally, I give women two opportunities during a lifetime when they can truly have a chance to enjoy a monogamous relationship. This is when you catch a man in the early stages, as a very young man, who maybe only has sex for the first time. Or as an older man who has learned the ways of a relationship, that the grass is not always greener on the other side. But I'm sorry, Ladies. Anything in between is a sixty-forty shot at a monogamous relationship.

The implication society gives us today is that a woman should basically turn her head and look the other way. Unfortunately, most women live by this creed—the women who want to hang onto the relationship that they choose to accept this way of life.

Now, I am in no way (as I have stated before) condoning anything I am writing in this book. I am merely stating the facts of life, as they exist today. Men have this justifiable, unspoken rule that is supposed to make it okay to cheat; family members, her girlfriends, neighbors—these are all supposed to be women that are offlimits. Long-term relationships with these outside women are unacceptable, but one-night stands can usually blow over. The biggest taboo is to have a child outside of the relationship; 90 percent of the time, this will not blow over and is never acceptable.

The mature man will understand that none of these things are acceptable to a woman.

The mistake that men make living by these unspoken rules is that they fail to place themselves in their woman's position. As I stated earlier in this chapter, men fail to realize the actual pain placed upon a woman's heart when she finds out he has slept with another woman. Yes, though it was unimportant and meaningless to the man, she cannot understand that reasoning at all. This starts the argument, "Baby, she didn't mean anything to me. It was a mistake. I slipped up. I was drunk."

She is not hearing any of these things, for the pain that we inflict on her heart in that moment she finds out is truly unbearable for her. A man who loves his woman can look deep into her eyes and will be able to not only see, but feel the pain she is experiencing, and at that moment, put yourself in her place and you may begin to understand that cheating is a bigger issue than we may put emphasis on.

One of the funniest things I have learned over my years is that women can be so loyal to her man that we don't even understand how she does it. In my younger years, I have met women who I know were feeling me as much as I was feeling them, but would not cross that line of going to bed, even though their man might be in the armed service and not coming home for months, or maybe incarcerated and not coming home for years. Yet though they were enjoying my company, no matter how much I tried to convince her, she would not cross that line. Can men make the same claim?

I posed questions to people who I knew, and even random ones off the street. And the question was this: What would you do if you found out your man/woman was cheating? Most of the answers I received from women seem to always leave the door cracked a little bit for a man to apologize his way back in. Some responses were, "I'd stay in a relationship if we had kids," "I'd try to find out why he did it and then probably break up," and "Find out the reason why he cheated and then work it out." But the most common answer I got was, "I probably don't know."

Now the same question was posed to the men, and the answers revealed how different we really are.

There were responses like, "I'd stay with her and treat her like a dog," "I'd cheat on her, too," and "I would confront the both of them together." But the most alarming and chilling answer I got was, "I would kill her." Now, as I talk to these men about this question and being a man myself, I could look in their eyes and presume they were probably already cheating or have definitely cheated in the past, as I have. But there was no way they were going to accept their woman cheating on them. This is the mentality of males and females involved in relationships. Society has allowed men to convinced themselves that they can still be a good husband and father and still cheat.

Even our former president, Bill Clinton, has infused another excuse for men that is now commonly being accepted, and that is that oral sex is not cheating. So where does the cheating line begin?

In this new age with so much technology, cheating is more prevalent than ever. Is intimate phone chat cheating? Is chatting on the Internet, looking at porn Web sites, or watching porn videos cheating? Going to a strip club, as long as you don't kiss on the mouth, or as long as your partner doesn't see you with their own eyes, are these things cheating? The opinion differs from person to person. It seems everyone makes their own ground rules where cheating is concerned.

Some women are even more responsible than the man for causing them to cheat. Sometimes a man may open up to a coworker or another type of female friend about what he's experiencing at home with no intention at all of cheating. But when a man opens up his feelings to another woman, he makes himself vulnerable for the allure of temptation, for discussing deep emotions and intimate issues almost always lead to sex.

As I stated, I do not have answers to many of the questions this book may present. It is not designed to provide answers; I am only stating the true reality of things. But let me reiterate, since women ask this question the most, maybe they should look back in the very beginning and ask themselves, who really changed, was it him or was it me?

4

The Insecurity Syndrome

One of the most detrimental reasons relationships fail is what I call the insecurity syndrome. This trait is found mostly in women, but there are men who carry this, too. This is a very serious problem, not to be taken lightly, especially when it pertains to a woman. Usually, this seed is planted at a very early age, typically due to abandonment by her father or a father figure. That abandonment leaves a scar on a little girl that you cannot possibly imagine.

Most don't display this insecurity, but it will emerge once a relationship with a man is established.

She will carry this insecurity into all future relationships, especially when she falls in love.

Though the man may not be aware of how deep this can run (and it varies from woman to woman), he must take this as serious as she does. Most men blow this off as hysterics she is displaying, but to her, all this pain and fear is very real.

This insecurity could begin to drive a wedge between the couple, especially if the man is not guilty of doing anything. He will begin to try to convince her that there is nothing going on. And particularly if there isn't, this will begin to nag at them both. She will swear that he's trying to make her crazy, while he will begin to realize there's no way to get through to her. It is not really either's fault, but till you to really sit down and communicate, it will cause the problem to manifest. He needs to understand that what she has been through in her past is now affecting their present.

Sometimes, the wound is so deep that it cannot be repaired, and now he must decide how much he loves her and can he continue to cope with this. An insecure woman who has deeply been affected by a broken home will always suspect everything her man is doing—phone calls, errand runs, and even simple things like hanging out with friends.

Now the ball is totally in the man's court; he will have to decide if this something he can live with for the rest of his life. Even the most patient man will become worn down trying to constantly explain something that doesn't exist. In defense of women, God has given them something very special, which, I think, they take too lightly, and that is a woman's intuition. Nine out of ten times, a woman may out of nowhere begin to feel something is just not right in her relationship. This intuition, I hate to admit, is usually right. Men have not figured out yet that when you are involved in a relationship, there is some kind of link that happens, and when they begin to stray, a woman may feel it immediately without any evidence or proof.

The thing is, though, how the woman conducts this gift of intuition. It periodically comes on; that's when it is probably accurate. But the woman who has it on all the time, always accusing, nagging, suspecting, is not able to take advantage of this sixth sense because she is stuck in this mode all the time.

Throughout time, men have always thought that they could get away with cheating. But once you take the time and get into a woman's feelings and her mind, and she into yours, you will realize you can't ever get away with it.

Her intuition will snitch you out every time, leaving a man with his only defense: denial.

They may not be able to prove it, but they know, and if they can't prove it, that seems to be good enough for men to continue to deny.

A man's insecurity may stem from many things. Just as a woman may suspect things going on at work, going out on errands, or just plain hanging out with his friends, a man can be just as accusing—except for one thing: an insecure man tends to be violent and controlling. It cannot be pleasant for a woman living in this situation. These men tend to embarrass their woman in public without a thought of rational thinking. He begins to accuse her of sleeping with everyone, from the mailman to his best friend.

Usually, these women are too afraid to even think about cheating, and he is too insecure to even realize that.

Slowly but surely, friends begin to fall away, she begins to socialize fewer and fewer times, she can barely talk on the phone to friends or family members even—all out of fear of being accused of something that she may not even be doing. In some cases, this insecurity will backfire on the insecure party. The accused may begin to act on these accusations, just because of the fact that he or she is being punished for a crime he or she didn't commit. So the rational thinking becomes, why not commit the crime since you'll be paying the price anyway?

A man's insecurity is truly a whole different ball game because abuse, both physically and verbally, is now introduced into the relationship, with a man ending up hitting and beating a woman for things she hasn't even done. But those things are real only in his mind; unfortunately, this type of man may also kill a woman.

The life expectancy of a relationship founded on insecurities is nil. You are only awaiting the pain, agony, and torment this relationship has in-store for you, because that's the only thing it has to offer.

5

Honey, We Need to Talk

"Honey, we need to talk," is probably one of the most feared statements that can fall upon a male's ear. Now being male, I'll probably come off a little chauvinistic on this subject, but I'm willing to accept it. This sentence usually comes up at the most inappropriate times, and most times, it means trouble is on the horizon. It'll usually come at you in a subtle, soft, unassuming tone. But these very words can sometimes end up in a hurricane of an argument, taking you places you have no idea how you got there, or why you're discussing something that happened eons ago.

Men are so often caught off guard that once they've open their mouths to respond it's too late, they are now swept in, trapped into a conversation that's sure to make them wish they'd rather be anyplace else in the world but right there and then. The words themselves are so powerful it could dredge up anything, and I mean things from the deep, dark past, to something here in the present. Or as crazy as it sounds, something she believes will occur in the future.

Here is where most women who are reading this will probably consider me a chauvinist, but what most men don't understand (and most women will deny) is that most of the time, women are really not in it for a solution—she's in it for the fight. What I mean is, at certain times, women just need that bantering back and forth, not looking for any plausible reason or solution, but just the flight itself.

Now I doubt very much if I could get any woman to admit to this fact, but I do have a surefire way of proving my point. Let a man try diffusing any argument right at the beginning. Listen intently to what she's saying, analyze it, and agree with her. I guarantee you are not getting off that easy, oh no.

This will only cause the conversation to begin to bounce around to all kinds of different other subjects, because you are not getting off with a short argument like that just because you agreed. By the time the man runs the whole gauntlet with her, he's usually left standing dizzy and bewildered, wondering how they traveled from the mortgage conversation to the Fourth of July picnic two years ago.

Men have to face the fact that this comes along as part of the relationship. There are just times when a woman wants to just discuss whatever pops into her head, and if you're not willing and capable of dealing with this, you are definitely not ready for anything long term. There is no diversionary tactic that you can try when she is in that mode. The best thing you can do is strap on your seat belt and prepare to go on that ride. Your one hope is to pray to God that it's a short ride!

Remember, when a female is in this mode, it is never the solution that she is after—it's the action of the fight itself. No rational point you're going to make, no agreeing with any wisdom she spews, no "Baby, can we talk about this later?" is going to work.

Take heed when you hear the sentence "Honey, we need to talk," because it does not mean let's solve a problem that we currently have. For a man, the translation is: I'm ready to push a few of your buttons for a while.

Now, I myself will admit this is one chapter in the book that probably does sound very chauvinistic, but I really wonder, is a woman reading this and saying to herself deep inside that, yes, this chapter is right on.

I think this is one of those woman things that they keep secret in their women club that men just have to learn to deal with. I guess it comes along with the whole package.

Look, it's like this. It doesn't matter how simple the solution is. No matter how many times you tell her it's black, she's going to say it's white. Not because she really thinks it's white, but simply because you said it's black. No matter how many times you say up, she is going to say down; no matter how many times you say right, she is going to say left.

Remember, Men, you have just got to learn to understand. Sometimes, it's just not about the solution—it's about the argument itself. Enjoy!

6

Abuse

Any form of this word connected to any type of relationship is doomed to fail, period. Nothing positive will ever come out of any relationship that has any form of abuse involved in it. Abuse is not something that can easily be fixed if it exists, and the only reason it does exist in some relationships is because one party is allowing it to—usually, with the mixed-up thinking that she can change the person, or that it will get better.

There are many ways abuse becomes part of a relationship. The sad fact of the matter is that it's sometimes the foundation of some relationships. With abuse as the foundation, it will usually have two partners who are both sick, because for people to need to abuse other people, whether it be verbally, mentally, or physically, they are sick themselves.

If one allows herself to be abused and continue to make excuses for the abuser, then she has issues usually stemming from low self-esteem due to some deep-seated upbringing. Either way, this is a very sick and sad relationship. Let's take a look at how abuse affects both of the sexes.

Abusers usually think that they are not abusive, justifying their actions by blaming their deeds on the other person, usually stating they were made to do this.

If you live with a person who spews continual negative remarks such as "You're fat," "You're worthless," "You're ugly," "You're stupid," refers to you as the "B" word, or make such comments as "You'll never amount to anything without me," "Nobody will ever want you," or "You can't do anything right"— then I'm sorry to be the one to tell you, but you are living with a verbally abusive person, one who is not likely to change. People who stay in this sort of relationship justify this by believing that their partner is just trying to better them. In reality, they are tearing down their self-esteem.

If you live with a person who strikes you, then he is a physically abusive person. This type of abuse usually creeps in very subtly. You may be into an argument, and then that first proverbial slap comes across your face, followed quickly by an apology that it will never happen again.

This is a *testing ground*, because if this is allowed to pass, the floodgates will now be open and you can bet there is more and worse to come no matter what he says. The worst thing I've ever heard an abuser tell the object of the abuse is that he did it because he loves her—love does not hurt physically. By not retreating after the first hit, you have set yourself up for far worse beatings as long as you are in the relationship.

The abuser now knows that you will forgive him for anything that he does, for if you take it the first time, you will take it the next time. The first time is the time to get out no matter how much you think you're in love. The funny thing is that most women don't. They find the craziest reasons (which I don't even understand) to hang on.

Some stay for the sake of children and family, some say that it was their fault, some swear he didn't mean it. Wake up! This situation is not about to change. In fact, it is about to get worse. This I can promise you. For if this person is telling you he loves you and is now begging you to believe that he didn't mean to strike you, and not just only once but at other times as well, then he is not sorry—he is sick.

You know, when you're into a relationship and abuse is present, don't let your emotions cloud your judgment, don't make excuses for what you know is staring you right in the face. The earlier you get out, the quicker you will have selfpreservation. You will find someone else. You will be able to make it with your children. You will be able to stand on your own two feet. You will surprise yourself once you remove yourself from the situation. What will *not* happen in an abusive relationship is that it will get better—an abuser is an abuser is an abuser.

We are living in a society today where abuse is almost an acceptable part of life—and that should not be, it's crazy. With all the violence that we face today in movies, music, video, and the Internet, society is swimming upstream, trying to combat the acceptance of abuse. If this chapter helps just one person to open her eyes and take a hard look at the situation, seeing it for what it really is and is able to get out, then I thank God.

Now, we will begin to get into the meat of things in this section of the book You get in where you fit in!

7

Fatal Attractions

We all know the meaning of the words "fatal attraction." But how many of us have actually lived through one? How many of us know how deadly it can really be?

Even if you've never experienced this situation (and court your blessings), living in this new age of technology, you can find the horrifying results of this chapter anywhere. It's all over the Internet, in our movies, in our reality TV shows, and worst of all, in our daily news broadcasts.

The danger is real. The majority is committed by men, but women have their moments, too. Men may commit murder, but women, usually revenge.

The real questions are: How do you know when you have a fatal attraction? What are the telltale signs?

For one thing, the reason people get caught up in fatal attractions is that they let their emotions blind them to the earlywarning signs these kinds of people give off. They are either so infatuated or deeply in love that they cannot see the trees beyond the forest. As they say, love is blind—in these cases, fatally blind.

Any time you get involved with someone who ends up going everywhere you have to go, calling you every time you're not in his or her presence, begins to alienate you from your friends and family, then there may be a problem.

Now, if you're smart enough to detach yourself from this situation, and still that person begins to show up at your job or at your house, calls continually, and jealous over the fact you have someone new, then you *do* have a problem!

The scary thing is that too many of these situations end in death. These days, it just seems that a partner will take your life in a heartbeat rather than see you live one without him or her. In this callous world we live in now, society barely looks twice at a domestic death. And to add insult to injury, the killer may end up seeing the light of day again at a later time due to our court system. Only the family of the lost love one is left with the fallout.

Meanwhile, the rest of us move on.

Most of the time, this is male-on-female fatal attraction. But women get in this mode, they become some of the most vindictive and vicious creatures on the face of the earth.

There is no limit to the damage they will inflict, from destroying personal property to bringing harm right into your home life.

We all witnessed Glenn Close in the movie, take it to heart.

FEMALES

1

Miss P.M.S.

Ooo, a real touchy subject here, huh? Well, any guy who's been in a relationship, whether it be a loving one, family related, or even work, school, etc. has met Miss P.M.S.

I'm only going to touch on the relationship aspect of this matter, though. Miss P.M.S. is the other woman—and I don't mean that in the good sense.

P.M.S. is so important an issue in a relationship that a man should not rightfully make a long-term commitment until he has met this other woman at least three or four times, and knows he is able to live with her.

And I'm not joking! Granted, it depends on the woman. Some have worse times than others. But they are all discomforted by this, which, in turn, is going to cause the male some discomfort, believe it.

Now any man who has been involved in even a semi-long relationship has got to learn about his woman at this time of the month. A man who is really attuned to his girl will know the week before her time of the month comes— in some cases, even realizing it's about to happen before she even does!

Take into consideration the fact that this chemical change in her is not her fault. So therefore, a good man will adjust accordingly. There are certain needs of hers that have to be met. Patience is definitely a virtue.

She needs that extra attention and understanding, a shoulder to cry on, a sympathetic ear. Catering to a few of her whims will make your week a lot more peaceful.

Now the penalty for not doing these things I have mentioned above may be a price you do not wish to pay!

Let us remember how much the emotional imbalance is amped up to the tenth power during that week, Guys! The crying at the drop of a dime, the mood swings that seem to occur every hour on the hour. But the worst is that the female feels so miserable she turns violent and vicious.

The things that she can spew out her mouth are like venom. If this special week is really bad for her, it can make her physically violent.

To be able to get along during this period (no pun intended) is a two-way street. The man has got to understand that this change is not her fault but an act of nature. The woman also has to come to the realization that she is acting erratic and needs to pull it in as much as she possibly can. And these two things have to occur numerous times throughout the week just to survive it!

Not every woman have bad P.M.S. so do not stereotype. But they all will suffer some sort of change to their natural character. Find out early on what these changes entail and know that you are able to live with them.

P.M.S. has destroyed relationships in the past, and it will destroy some more in the future. It's not a part of life that a man should take lightly.

2

Miss Submissive

Miss Submissive refers to the female who pretty much allows any and everything to go on in a relationship. This female usually displays a sense of low self-esteem, which prevents her from standing up for what she believes in. She will allow anything from her man—the cheating, the beating, the yelling, the degrading at her, etc.

A submissive woman will know that her man is having affairs with other women, but she will just turn the other cheek and pretend that what she knows does not really exist. As her man steps out on her night after night and day after day, any excuse that he chooses to serve her she will just accept and continue to move on in a somewhat blinded fashion. The only problem is that this sense of blindness is not created from a natural act or accident; it is one she creates so as to not feel so weak.

Even when a submissive woman is being beaten on a regular basis, she will just make up excuses for the bruises that she may display, or even worse, begin to say she is at fault for the actions or her abuser. If the relationship has only escalated to a verbal abusive standpoint, she will accept all the criticism rendered her way, though underneath, she may even know that these things said to her are not true.

She will not stand up for any decisions made about the children (if there are any involved). Even though she may be the mother who is home continually with the child, day after day, and probably knows better how the child will react to a certain situation, she will stay quiet about the decision her significant other might makes.

A submissive woman who is paired with the wrong mate will eventually find herself isolated from her family, friends, coworkers, and sometimes, maybe even her children. Gradually, she will lose all sense of her own thoughts and ideas, totally relying on a man's decisions, unable to make a single move if he's not around or formulate her own plans and ideas without his input. She has become a shell of the person she used to be, and usually, this is exactly what her male counterpart had set out to achieve.

The way out for a submissive woman, who is in an unappreciative relationship, is to stand up. This is much easier said than done for her, but if she does not, the submissiveness could gradually deteriorate into plain out slavery. She has got to trust what she believes in her heart, and once she is confident that she is right, she must not let go of her standpoint, no matter how tough the battle may become.

If she can achieve this for the first time, she will get stronger and stronger until she is able to battle her way back and become a 50 percent entity in the relationship. And if she can do this, she must never let it go and never back up. Now, I'm not saying this as if I thought it is a simple solution. You must sympathize with the submissive woman; you don't know what happened in her childhood that brought her self-esteem to such a low point. But I want to say that I do believe if this is you, you can change.

Make up your mind that you have had enough, and stop accepting any and everything he serves you; if you don't feel right, speak your mind. For if the relationship has reached this point, what have you really got to lose?

No, I'm not saying there's anything wrong with being a submissive woman. I am just saying it's okay to be submissive to a man who appreciates you for it, who does not take advantage of the fact that you love to bring him dinner, clean his house, watch his kids, rub his back. To the men who have these types of women (especially in this day and age), stop being so stupid and appreciate and thank God for what you have.

Oh, by the way, don't forget to show her from time to time how much you do appreciate her, or someone else just might!

3

Mrs. Bossy

Mrs. Bossy usually refers to that special type of woman who feels she has been born with certain genitals. Now in my opinion, and in my opinion only (and if I'm lucky, maybe a few other people as well), I believe in the old-school ways, that a man is a man is a man, and a woman who's a woman is a woman. Granted changes have occurred in society and through liberation movements, which has modified these standards somewhat, and I have no personal problem with that.

But I do believe (in my somewhat little male chauvinistic way) that a line has to be kept to allow a man to be a man. Yes, her opinions should be considered at all times, and most of the time, I do believe a man who is truly for her and the family is going to have the more accurate opinion. But that is not to say that sometimes we are wrong and should not be too manly not to admit it and go with her suggestion. Someone has to be the more levelheaded in moments of crisis, and that should be the man, but only if his history and relationship has been continually smart and beneficial.

Now most of the time, what we find in this new day and age is a constant power struggle between the two. Rather than the pair trying to resolve a very difficult situation, a man can find that, being paired with a bossy woman, she is not really looking for a solution at all, but rather, for an opportunity to seize the chance at tipping the scales of power in her favor no matter how irrational her suggestion might be. If you are dealing with a bossy woman, you'll find that her real goal is to just suggest the opposite of what you're saying in an effort to be in control.

I further believe that this has led to the increase of lesbianism that we now accept in our society. If a bossy woman cannot get a man she can control, you can find that she will choose a female companion in order to have that same dominating power that a man traditionally holds in a relationship.

Don't get it twisted, though. Some women need to be bossy due to their choice of men. This man usually has no, what we call today, backbone. He is the type of man who may be considered wimpy or insecure (this we will be covered when we get into the male section of the book). If a man is too weak to take control of the important and vital situations that arise either in his family or his relationship, then someone has to step up to the plate. This does not make this type of woman a bossy woman, but one who does what needs to be done.

But we will stick with the topic of this chapter, and that is Mrs. Bossy. These women secretly wish that they had a penis. Why? Having a penis does not make one a man, but I believe they think that if they had one they would feel more in control, or at least entitled to take control. If you are really a man's man, you will not last too long with the Mrs. Bossy. This type of relationship will eventually wear you down. Instead of finding more time to enjoy each other, you will find that you are spending time in a constant competitive battle to seize power, which you really do not choose to be a part of.

You'll never be able to reach Mrs. Bossy because she has a single goal, and that is to change and control her man. She is unable to see the light at the end of the tunnel, which is the solution to a certain problem that has arisen in the relationship— and it could be child related, business related, work related, or relationship related. Because though the man is usually focused on rectifying the problem that has arisen, her focus will totally be on making sure she gets her way, even at the cost of making the problem much bigger.

How do you know if you have a Mrs. Bossy? Well, when you begin to feel as if you have to answer for every move that you make; every time your answer is up, her answer will be down; and every time you say black, her response will be white. Now don't fool yourself. You are not in control of anything. I have used this word "control" many times throughout this chapter, but it may be a poor choice of word because I really don't believe in one human being having the authority to control another. Slavery is over, isn't it?

The real key is to work on things together; sometimes it's your way, sometimes it's her way. But the main focus should be to get the right way, and not turning every crisis or problem into a battle for control. When I say that the man should be in control, this is only on the premise that he knows what the hell he is talking about and has guided the relationship or the family through troubled waters before and has been successful. If he has done this on numerous occasions, Mrs. Bossy needs to take a backseat for a minute and allow him to do his thing, letting him feel like a man in taking pride in the fact that he has secured a solution for a problem, not only for himself but also for the two of them.

Another place Mrs. Bossy seems to raise her overbearing ways is in public. There is nothing worse than having a woman scold a man in public, as if he were a little child. Mrs. Bossy doesn't care who's there or where she is; her point is going to be made. How many times have you seen some woman come down to some guy's job and blast him out even if there were clients or customers present? And while she's going on and on you're asking yourself, doesn't she realize these people are staring? The answer: she doesn't care.

She's there to put you in check and let you know your place, let you know who the boss is!

There are other ways to detect signs of a Mrs. Bossy. She will not only display this mannerism in a relationship, but also at her place of work, at family gatherings, or even at organization events. So know the signs before you claim, "She's mine!"

4

Miss Argumentative

Miss Argumentative refers to the kind of woman who's going to find an argument every day of the week, no matter how trivial or big the problem may be. This is going to be the kind of woman who you would be in a supermarket with while you're perusing the groceries; she'll start a big argument, claiming you were staring at another woman down the aisle. This is the kind of woman who will start an argument over matters that don't even pertain to her, the kind of woman who will drag you into an argument over the neighbor's business.

You see, for her it's never about getting to a specific point. Arguing seems to be her life's blood; she needs to argue the way people need to breathe. You wake up in the morning and your day kind of goes like this: she begins to argue because you opened the blinds and it's too bright outside; now she argues you're taking too long in the bathroom, and continues arguing that your breakfast is getting cold—and there's your morning.

Now you're at work and a cell phone begins to ring, and for whatever reason, she's calling to argue about something else, and this is only call number one of about ten calls you will receive throughout the day. You could not even agree with this woman just to cease the argument, because she will just switch gears— and subjects—to keep it going.

Check this out, and this is mostly pertaining to the men, about how women have this uncanny knack for tinkering around in your space and making it seem so innocent. It goes something like this: You have your own routine about where you put your things on the nightstand, maybe in the bathroom or maybe on the desk. But you have a certain order, and you do the same things the same way all the time. One day, you come home and you're looking for a certain item that you use all the time and always put in the same area.

Now you're the only two people in the house, and suddenly, your item is misplaced. You question her about it and you get this deer-in-the-headlights kind of look, and she responds, "Whaaaat?" So she doesn't know what you're talking about. You both begin to look around, and suddenly, you find what you're looking for in the most awkward place in the house, a section you haven't been in over six months.

Or maybe you're in bed, and she just can't sleep unless her arm is over you, or a leg, or some other appendage that has to be protruding into your area.

Trust me, Men, these little things are just ways to get a little rise out of you. That's bait set out for you to take and open a door for a good argument.

You are never ever going to change this woman. She is not seeking love, family, or any of the normal aspects of a relationship.

She feeds off the argument. She needs this. It's her sustenance in life, so you either learn to live with it or leave it alone. There is no middle ground. That's argument territory.

5

Miss Home Wrecker

This chapter is one that perplexes even me. Why does it seem that some women will go to great lengths to sabotage another women's relationship?

Women can be so vicious to one another, its plain scary. Men are supposed to be the dogs, but a female will make a deliberate effort to try and seduce her girlfriend's, sister's, cousin's, and, in some cases, mother's boyfriend! And in all honesty, most men fall headfirst into this trap.

Now, I'm not here to judge the man (this will come up in later chapters), but to try and find out exactly what Miss Home Wrecker's goals are. I know one of the main excuses is jealousy, but this is a family member, or a friend so close she could be family.

Being a male, I can't even pretend I know the answers. Other than the jealousy factor, I believe each woman has her own personal agenda. But the way they can hurt each other with such careless recklessness is truly mean.

Not excusing the male for his part in it, but a man doesn't usually go after another guy's girl, unless she somehow invites him to.

It's hard for me to elaborate on this particular chapter because I would have to know the heart and mind of the home wrecker to pinpoint her exact motivation. Let me assure you, though, that a woman knows exactly what she's doing and what her intentions are from the very outset!

I guess this is a woman thing that men will never understand. But, Men, beware—because in most cases like this, after the destruction has been done, that woman will be long gone, leaving you alone and with nothing!

6

Miss Crazy (with a K)

I'm about to make one of the most chauvinistic remarks I could make in this book. All women are crazy! But there are different degrees.

What I really mean to say is women are the most emotional creatures walking this planet. Between hormone changes, P.M.S., love, and all the rest of the basic emotions humans carry, females do not handle many of these situations well.

The trick for men is to find what degree of craziness he can withstand and learn to love and adjust accordingly. Women can get angry all they want, but if they're true to themselves, they know what I am writing is correct.

Now don't get me wrong, there is a level that resembles normalcy; all women aren't overly dramatic and erratic. But boy, the ones who are—watch out. I'm not going to sit here and bash women on this issue; I'm really referring to their emotional stability when I use the word crazy. Maybe I shouldn't even be using the word at all.

But I'm sorry, there is one out there who deserves the title and wears it with pride. This is Miss Crazy with a K!

Miss K comes in all shapes, sizes, and nationalities. This woman is over-the- top dramatic, somewhat psychotic, and could be a danger to you, as well as herself, under the right circumstances. In all fairness, this type of woman probably bears deep emotional scars that she has never learned to deal with. This can stem from so many things that unless she is able to tell you directly, you would never figure it out; thus, it is why most men end up using the phrase, "She's just crazy."

A woman fitting into this category goes to the extreme in almost all situations she finds herself in, and when she is upset, all hell could break loose.

When this fury is directed at a man, she will go as far as to stalk him, key his car, smash his windows, spread untruths about him, or threaten him or someone close to him. It is not beyond her to physically attack him or someone close to him, or even do herself harm.

The problem is that this woman does not show her true self until triggered by some kind of emotional event, then she goes totally out of control. No matter what you say when she is in this state, there is no reaching her. And the episode may not subside for hours.

When this anger is directed at children, unfortunately, it usually results in child abuse. The funny thing is that this woman is capable of controlling these outbursts of rage in public. What happens is she works so hard at concealing her true self that when it explodes, it seems she has just gone nuts. The outbursts of rage are usually saved for someone close to her, probably someone who is always there to help her, but ends up taking the lashing. The pent-up rage is almost always vented at an undeserving person.

Remember, though, that this woman has deep issues. In relationships, most men don't bother to explore what may be really troubling her and, therefore, chalk it up to craziness. But that's not really the case at all.

It could stem from a deep-seated father issue, molestation, some form of abuse, abandonment, betrayal, low self-esteem, bipolar disease, etc.

Women are up against a lot more than men from the time of their birth till they die, and let me be the first to say that I do sympathize with Miss K; I just don't know how to deal with her.

MALES

1

Mama's Boy

The female who's dealing with a mama's boy has really got her hands full. In all honesty, she is fighting a losing battle.

There are two situations that pertain to a mama's boy. First is the fact that the mother will always be in control of her son no matter what the relationship entails, be it kids, marriage, or whatever the case.

The other is that the man will never stand up and let the apron strings loose. The interfering-mother scenario is one that is a real pain to a woman. No matter what she does or what she puts out with, she will never measure up to her partner's mother's standards. She will be criticized and persecuted to the fullest extent every time she turns around, and her partner will not stand up to his mom and defend her.

His tactic will be to try and smooth things over, all the while protecting and agreeing with his mom. If he still lives at home, the chances of getting him to move out are almost nil. Mom is most likely still cooking his meals, washing his clothes, cleaning his room, etc.

Even if his partner is also providing these same things, they will not be as good as the way Mom does them, in Mom's eyes and in his eyes.

Your cooking can be delicious but not quite as good as Mom's; your house is never as clean as hers.

Troy E. Williams

And oh boy, if children are involved, this can turn the situation really ugly. Just as Mom shelters and smothers her son, his partner will be inclined to do the same for the children they have now produced together. And the last thing in the world she wants to hear is his mom telling her how to raise their children.

This will cause an automatic rift in the relationship, usually leading the female to force the male into a decisive situation— she and the kids or Mama!

This scenario has broken many a home. The overbearing mother, or the weak mama's boy, does not realize the ramifications of the decision, or just does not care, leading another mother to end up a single parent, of which we have too many cases of in the world as it is.

My sympathy goes out to these women in this situation. They are most likely deeply in love with these men, hoping beyond all hope that they will be able to break free from the apron strings. But sometimes, even in the event of his mom's death, the strings remain intact, and now the women will be fighting the ghost of his mom's ways.

These mama's boys just can't or won't change! Being dominated and reared by their moms all their life, they have no sense of self, and it doesn't seem that any female companion will be able to give them any, either.

Dealing with the weak plain-out mama's boy, who doesn't necessarily have the dominating mother, is another kind of frustration all its own.

This type of man can't make any decisions on his own; will not take the initiative to do anything on his own. The female will always find herself wearing the pants in this relationship, always leading him around by the hand. Eventually, this becomes frustrating for her, as most women like their man to be a man, who takes the lead and makes the hard decisions along with her, not leaving the ball in her court all the time.

He becomes like another child for her to raise, always waiting around for her to tell him what to do, what to wear, when to leave, where to go, and even who he is!

At this late stage in his life, there is no probability for him to change. His partner may believe she has what it takes to change him, she may even think the love they share will be enough to bring him around, but the sad fact of the matter is that it is what it is.

Face it, Ladies, anybody out there dealing with a mama's boy better realize the fact that in order for you to make that kind of relationship work, you better learn how to become his mama!

2

The Lazy Man

The lazy man, where do I begin? My first and foremost question pertaining to this type of male is how the hell does he even end up with a woman? I mean nothing personal against the guy, but what the heck does a woman find to love in an absolutely lazy bum of a man?

I guess in this chapter, rather than expounding my worldly wisdom, I'll find myself asking more questions than giving answers and advice.

The only realistic reasoning for a woman to tolerate a lazy bum probably has to do with her maybe having low self-esteem and severe lack of self- confidence.

Now when I talk about the lazy man, I'm referring to some of the most unbelievable tolerances a woman could ever endure. This woman does everything, and I do mean everything! She cooks, cleans, raises the kids, takes out the trash, does the yard, paints the house, does the laundry, goes shopping, irons, pays the bills, goes to work, does the dishes, nurses the family back to health, and then provides sex at the end of the day, every day!

All the while, this man is lying around the house, or posted up on the couch, with his hand down his pants, drinking, smoking, getting high, or something to that effect.

What in the world makes a woman stand by a guy like that, low self-esteem, insecurity, fear? Your guess is as good as mine. I said earlier in this book that I didn't have the answers to everything, just the truth. But the women out there who are putting up with this type of man are living an empty, one-sided relationship. This type of man does not love his woman; she is just a convenience for him, becoming more like a mother than a significant other.

This man is never going to change his ways. They say you can't teach an old dog new tricks. Well, you have an old lazy dog, and he doesn't want to learn new tricks!

A woman can detect the first signs that she is in a relationship like this from the outset. It starts out like she's just taking care of her man, catering to his needs.

As time goes on, this catering slowly develops into a form of spousal slavery. The more she does for him, the less he does— period. This daily routine gradually becomes the norm, and what is established in the beginning of a relationship becomes the foundation. As it progresses, it becomes too late to change down the road.

There is just not much to elaborate on this subject; it is what it is. So if you have one of these lazy men in your life, Ladies, you either learn to live with it and love it or find yourself something new. There is no change coming, nor any middle ground to stand on. Good luck!

3

The Control Freak

ere is one of the most scariest men in this book. The confidence and bravado he displays is all false. In truth, he is the most insecure, low self-esteemed man you can find. His actions toward his women reveal his true lack of confidence.

The things this kind of man will put his companion through are utterly insane. And any women out there who are tolerating this kind of treatment better wake up fast before the situation escalates into something fatal.

Myself being a man, I cannot believe some of the things these men can put a woman through. It starts out with him needing to know everywhere she is and every place she's going, calling her cell every ten or fifteen minutes to check on her. He is suspicious of any man she has contact with, including coworkers, her boss, delivery men, and store clerks—even suspicious of something as small as saying hi to a guy passing in the street.

These small things enrage a control freak and can result to physical abuse on the woman. Can you imagine being in her shoes? She can't really carry on a general conversation with a male coworker because of the fear she has of this person. And he doesn't even work there! She's riding along in a car with him and she accidentally make's eye contact with a passing motorist or pedestrian, and then suddenly, she finds herself being accused of wanting that man or having an affair with him. Imagine having to suffer that!

Not to mention the other crazy things she has to endure— like having her panties checked, getting herself sniffed, or undergoing a cell phone inspection. She has become property!

This man actually believes he owns her, tearing her self-esteem down so low that she believes it, too. He keeps her in a state of fear by doing degrading things to her, things you wouldn't even make a child do—like having her clip his toenails, run his bath, serve his food, wear only what he allows her to wear, speak only when told to, and walk with her head down as not to make any eye contact with anyone.

He shuts her off from her family and the world to maintain only his influence. She cannot formulate any type of opinion or idea for fear of being beaten or slapped. She isn't even allowed to work, trapped in a house like an actual prisoner, of which she is.

Understand why this man acts this way: he knows that if anyone or anything ever opens this woman's eyes or gives her any semblance of her real worth, she will see him for the weak, insecure boy he really is.

If a man can't hold a woman with love and respect, he cannot consider himself a man; he's lying to her and himself.

Why, in the beginning of this chapter, I called him one of the most scariest kind of male is because once he begins to lose his possessive hold on his woman, his own insecurities cause him to panic. He truly cannot function on his own and knows people will finally see him for what he really is: just a scared boy at heart.

Unfortunately for the female, when the control freak reaches this state of emotion, she can find herself in real danger. There are so many documented incidents of this type of men going off the deep end at this point, resulting in beatings, causing paralysis to her, and even the ultimate offense, killing her! Rather than lose her and face his own shortcomings, he will take her life before he lets her go and allow her to find her own self-worth.

Any woman finding herself in this kind of situation must discover a way out! It will neither change nor get better. The longer the relationship continues, the longer he will seek to gain more and more control over her life, and in the end, it will end badly for one of them. If he doesn't kill her, she may find herself behind bars for having to kill him in a self-defense situation, which sometimes the courts of our land don't find to be in her favor. Imagine a lifelong existence of being controlled and abused, and then ending up in a prison sentence. And it happens more often than we know.

There is no light at the end of these tunnels with a control freak. You have got to put that feeling of love for him aside at the first sign of a controlling behavior, and get out then and there. It's much better to have a broken heart early, than a broken neck later!

4

The Wimp

Okay, let's keep this one real. Would a woman really want a straight up wimpy man? I don't care how strong minded and secure a woman is; deep inside, she stills wants a man who can step up to the plate and take charge of a situation when called for.

Now don't get me wrong. I don't mean for him to overrule her, but what woman would want to make all the major decisions in a relationship?

A man who doesn't have a backbone really does not bring anything to the table in a relationship; the woman has to decide for the both of them—what to eat, what to wear, when to come, when to go. For her, it's like having another child to raise.

I often ponder the situation when I see a woman with a wimpy man. Is it insecurity, low self-esteem? Or maybe, in some cases, the woman has that male-complex thing going on and enjoys being the boss and having full control over her partner/family.

Other than that scenario, most women in this type of relationship are not truly happy deep down; perhaps they're just being tolerant. Maybe because of past bad relationships, they are content to settle with this man. Maybe they don't feel they can attract anyone different. Or maybe by having a wimpy man, they think they can insure monogamy on his part. But the truth of the matter is that it may backfire and she may find herself cheating, looking for that strong leadership she does not have at home.

It must be hard for a woman to be in a relationship like this. Basically, she's always propping up her partner in public to make him appear to be more than what he actually is, when in reality, without her he can barely stand on his own two feet.

In all honesty, there is not much I can write on this subject. I really do not know much about it. Why a woman would want to be with a man who cannot raise the gumption to make critical decisions where his family or his woman is concerned has always perplexed me.

This being the shortest chapter in the book is due to the fact that I have no real answers and cannot pass any judgment. All I can say is that a woman must have her own personal reasons why she would choose to be in such a one-way relationship. But the real question she must ask herself: is she truly happy?

5

The Player

The player was a term used in the late eighties, pertaining to a guy who had numerous women on the side of an already existing relationship. Today the term is called just what it is, a cheater.

A woman who stays in a relationship with a player/cheater dumbfounds me even more than the female who stays with a wimpy man.

A player is never ever going to be loyal to a woman no matter how much he claims to love her. Not only is he not going to be loyal, he has no morals or ground rules on his cheating escapades whatsoever. No female is off-limits to this type of man—her sisters, cousins, friends, coworkers, nobody!

The player will cheat at will with whomever and wherever the opportunity may present itself. He constantly lies and has excuses to his companion at every turn, and no matter what he says, Ladies, he is not going to change. Some players can't help it; his goal is to conquer as many females as possible.

The funny thing is that these men usually procure a steady relationship first, then commence to cheating at will. They will constantly lie to their partners as they pursue every skirt that crosses their paths. And these men cannot be trusted anywhere a female may be present, be it in a grocery store, family outing, on the street, at a job, even at a church. There is no sacred place to the player.

Women who have a player are blind to everything this man does. There's no way she doesn't know what's going on because he's so blatant about his activities. But he'll tell her the most ridiculous lies in the world and it will be enough for her to turn her head the other way.

I'm here to tell you, Ladies, that what you see is what you get! If you're staying in this kind of relationship hoping and waiting for him to change, you're only fooling yourself. Learn to live with it or move on.

The woman must learn to love herself and stop believing that someday he'll love her the way she's expecting to be loved. It's just never going to happen!

Being a man, I have been down this player road. The thing that a player/cheater doesn't stop to realize is the devastating pain he inflicts upon his woman every time he does it. Even though she may not be addressing these situations verbally when they happen, she is suppressing them deep inside. Trust me she knows and it hurts her.

I myself have found this out the hard way. I have many regrets about the women I have hurt. I can now say that I truly have sympathy for these women. Nine out of ten times, they don't let go. And if they do get out of the relationship, a lot of times they'll find themselves a man who treats them the same way.

I now have a twenty-two-year-old daughter myself, and as a father, I dread the possibility she could suffer that kind of hurt and pain. Maybe that's something all players/cheaters should think about: what if it was your little girl or sister being played?

THE CONCLUSION

1

The Good Man

To begin with, the good man will present himself truthfully at the very outset, when you meet him. He will not be afraid to let you know exactly how he is.

He's not the type of man who six months into the relationship, you're going to find out all these hidden secrets about him. He is confident in himself, not perfect (we all have our faults), but not ashamed to disclose his.

This, in turn, offers a good foundation for a relationship. Imagine knowing basically all the things you want to know about your man from the start, and for a change, it's all true—then being able to make a rationale decision on whether or not you want to get involved.

This man will also have the self-confidence needed to be a leader and protector of his family/partner. He will not be influenced or intimidated by outside sources, such as his job or his mom. He will know when and what to do in the best interest of himself and his family/partner.

He doesn't waver in his decision process. Even when they turn out wrong, he deals quickly and confidently with the situation, because even he will make mistakes along the way. But he won't be afraid to tell you of these mishaps, as he will want the both of you to work to rectify them.

Cheating will not be a part of his personality. You see, a good man is not born. Society offers so much corruption and

Troy E. Williams

temptation that a man is behind the eighth ball from birth. He has to learn to overcome these things in order to become this good man. This is acquired with wisdom and age, plus learning from mistakes as you go along in life.

I'm sorry, Ladies, but it's the rarest of cases when you'll find a man like this at an early age. In all truth, men just do not mature as fast as women. A lot of women will not like the next thing I'm about to say, but sometimes, it is best to look the other way. Not forever, but if she truly loves this man, she may have to tolerate a few things while he matures into the relationship. The trick, though, is to see if he is trying to grow and mature, or if he is just falling into a pattern of immaturity that will just continue for the entire duration. It's a very thin line and, I agree, not fair to the female, but nevertheless, it's real.

The good man will show these signs of maturity and monogamy early as the relationship progresses, especially as he makes mistakes. If a woman does not detect these changes, she is probably swimming against the tide and this guy will not grow into the good man.

Another thing a good man will do is listen. This seems to be one of the most major reasons relationships deteriorate. A man feels that a woman needs to talk all the time—and they do! But we, as men, cannot take this as light as we do. Even though most things women talk about seem irrelevant to men, understand this: it's very real and very important to them!

The good man will be a good listener. He does not just "uh huh" her, he hears and relates. This definitely comes with maturity. The last thing the average male wants to do is hear his woman begin to start yakking the minute he comes home. But if a woman has that good guy, he'll sit her down and try and understand—not always, but majority of the time.

On the subject of abuse, any woman knows that a good man does not abuse his woman in any way, shape, or form. He doesn't degrade or belittle her, doesn't break down her self-esteem. He lets her know on a daily basis how beautiful she is, because to him, it's not only about her physical beauty, but her inner beauty that keeps him in love.

You will not have to worry about him being a mama's boy, because he's the type of man who not only can take care of you but also looks out for his mama, too.

He goes to work, helps around the house, has a hand in raising the kids, and treats you like an equal.

When you're in a relationship that allows you the freedom to be who you are, to have the trust in someone to feel secure, and to have the foundation of honesty, then you are with a good man. Keep him and treat him well!

2

The Good Women

O kay, I'm going to try and be as fair as I possibly can. Writing this perspective from a standpoint of a man, I don't want to overdo it!

First off, the ideal good woman is going to present her true self the second you meet her. There will be no false representation or pretense about her. Her confidence will ooze to the point that if you're not a confident man, you may be intimidated.

A good woman is automatically instilled with monogamy. Nothing another man has or can offer will tempt her to stray. The love for her partner is infallible. This faithfulness even extends to the point where, if her man has to be gone for long periods of time, she will wait patiently and loyally. A man does not have to wonder what a good woman is doing no matter where he is or how long he is away.

Another thing a good woman does not do is constantly berate and belittle her man. This is one of the easiest ways to drive a man away, or into another woman's arms.

As I stated back in the Why He Cheats chapter, the reason a man may cheat is sometimes the woman's fault. Constantly dogging your man will wear at his self-esteem. Then should another female enter the picture with nothing but praise, admiration, and compliments for him, he may become susceptible to her compassion and charm.

The good woman is aware of this and does not create this type of opening for another woman to take advantage of.

She will also not exhibit any types of insecurities, whether it be of herself or any fears of what her man may be doing when not in her presence.

Even the good woman needs an understanding, sympathetic ear—all women do.

A good woman will be submissive to her partner, but only to a certain extant. Her submissiveness will allow him to be and feel like a man, but not to the point of demeaning herself.

She's not bossy, but firm in her issues. She works together with her partner, not against him.

All couples argue; it comes with the territory. But it's not the fact that you argue, it's how you handle the aftermath. A good woman can admit when she has been proven wrong, and that's a very big deal, as most women will not!

Of course, she is not a home wrecker. The minute she finds out the person she is interested in is involved with someone else, she's out.

And I will reiterate, when you're in a relationship that allows you the freedom to be who you are, to have the trust in someone to feel secure, and to have the foundation of honesty, then you are with a good woman. Keep her and treat her well!

3

The Good Relationship

The good relationship, wow, does it really exist anymore? You definitely can't title this chapter the perfect relationship. I'm pretty sure that's a thing of the past!

With just about everything in this world working against you, consider yourself blessed to have a good relationship. For one thing, our technology has superseded our humanity. Temptation abounds everywhere.

So how do you achieve the good relationship? I think we've got to go back to basics.

Communication and trust are the two true foundations to build upon. Without both of these factors intact, the relationship is a disaster waiting to happen, and it surely will! Communication is essential. Too many times as the relationship wears on, we lose our perspective on how important the other person's feelings and opinions are. We may not find them as important as our partner does, or maybe not even that interesting, but to have a good relationship, patience and consideration must be exercised.

How many times do we hear the joke from comedians about the man getting home from work and the wife starting right in on him? Though this might sound funny coming from the comedian, it'll turn out to be a very grim matter later down the road in your relationship if not taken seriously.

First of all know this, women need to talk. Whether it be meaningful to men or not, you've got to be attentive to these moments. Knowing from the start that women are emotional creatures, you have got to listen and put yourself in her position to truly try and understand.

The expression "men are from Mars and women are from Venus" could never be truer in the realm of conversation. Sometimes, talking to a woman can take you places during the conversation that'll have you warp speeding from place to place, back to the future, the land that time forgot, and any other place, date, or time she navigates the conversation to.

Your job is to listen, focus, and try to keep up! And I'm not talking about pacifying her, either.

Yeah, the good relationship is going to take a lot of work and effort, and I'm just getting started!

Now let's talk trust. Every couple will say you must have trust to make a relationship work. But saying it and exercising it are two different things. We cannot claim to trust our partners while at the same time rifling through their cell phone, checking their e-mails, tailing them when they leave home, calling constantly to find out where they are, questioning others about them, or the million other ways we spy on our partners while all the time saying, "Of course I trust you, Honey." No, you don't!

Yes, I stated early on all the temptations working against relationships in this day and age, and having to trust your partner is an enormous leap of faith, but one that must be added to the equation of a good relationship to establish one. We must trust our partners at their place of employment, public gatherings, and even when they venture into cyberspace.

Spending your time worrying or spying on them during these moments will for surely erode the relationship bit by bit.

Trust is opening up yourself from the very start. Don't pretend to be more than you actually are. The truth will just expose you later down the road, and you won't be able to live up to the standard you faked at the beginning. Be yourself—your partner will either take it or leave it!

To have a good relationship, both parties must respect one another. Your woman is not a live-in maid, day-care sitter, chef, or even a sex slave. She is your partner, fifty-fifty, and must be treated accordingly.

Don't wear down her self-esteem. Let her know how good she looks and how much you love her on a regular basis. Women need this, but you better mean it. Their intuition will detect whether you really are sincere or not.

Same goes for women. Don't constantly badger your man. You can't put him down every time he lifts his head up. Stop comparing him to other males you know—he's not them!

Men have a natural protective and support system built in; don't shoot down all his ideas and dreams. Try supporting him sometimes. Even if he fails, your support of him will go a long way to strengthening your relationship.

Allow him to be a man; too many women want to wear the pants.

It goes without saying that monogamy is a must for any good relationship. You cannot inflict the type of pain on one another that cheating causes and expect to sustain a long-term love life!

Do not let insecurity creep into your lives or the relationship, don't abuse each other (physically or verbally), discuss important decisions together, and do not try to dominate one another.

I told you, it takes a lot of work and effort to obtain and maintain the good relationship, and I'm not finished yet!

I know I've made a lot of references about women and their emotions. Please forgive me if it seems I went a little overboard, but I am writing from a male perspective. But I do have to stand by all the things I have said!

And on that note, let's discuss mood swings. To have that good relationship, you better prepare yourself for the inevitable mood swing! Oh, yes, this is definitely a component of a good relationship.

I'm not just talking about women here, either. That expression "you awoke on the wrong side of the bed" applies to men, too. As time goes on and you continually awake each morning with this same person, every morning will not be so cheerful. Even throughout the day, he or she may not shake that unpleasant mood that accompanied them. So what do you do? What you don't do is allow that mood to manipulate the day. Don't let it force you into meaningless arguments, causing you to not speak to one another for the entire day, sometimes even longer.

Learn to know your partner. Understand that this is not how they normally act. Give them that required space and let them come back to themselves, and then they will come back to you.

I mentioned arguing. Boy, can a relationship live without this, huh? But, unfortunately, it seems as though it can't. It's not that the good relationship is doomed because of arguing. It's not the fact that you argue. It's how you argue! It's a very thin line between arguing and disagreeing.

When you argue, and you *will* argue, the trick is to try and stay focused on the topic at hand. Don't start drifting off into past similarities of the subject; stay with the matter at hand. Listen to each other; contemplate what one another is saying. See if they may actually have a good point, or even the solution.

Don't allow yourself to be blinded to correcting the problem just because it wasn't your point. Another thing, avoid the namecalling. This will take you so far off track that you won't remember what the argument was about in the first place.

The key to resolving the argument is to talk about each other's reasoning and not your own every minute. Discuss his, and then discuss hers. With a clearer mind, a solution can be achieved— and a bitter battle avoided!

Another feared danger to the good relationship is the outside force. Never ever allow outside influences to interfere with your relationship. Women, I have to tell the blatant truth: never trust another female to be alone for long periods of time with your man. It doesn't matter who or what she is to you, it's a recipe for disaster.

First off, a woman who doesn't have that good relationship you have will have that automatic jealousy thing simmering deep within her and she will betray you. She may not even want to be with your man, but just to show you your relationship isn't as good as you've claimed.

Men, be smarter. Most of the time, this woman just wants to ruin your relationship. And let's tell the blatant truth here, too: men can't be trusted in an atmosphere where another woman is involved for long periods of time.

Sorry, but true. By nature, we are just too weak when it comes to the opposite sex.

Women, think about how you landed him. Could another woman entice him given the same scenario?

I'm not saying all men, all women, or even all relationships. But the blatant truth is that we are talking about the significant majority!

Again, lots of work, lots of effort, but it can be achieved. And if it is, it is well worth it. Who wants to be alone and not share all the accomplishments and great things life has to offer us?

Find someone who is willing to go the distance and is on the same page. Put in the work, and when you settle into that good relationship and time starts to roll on by, good times and bad, you'll be doing it with a smile on your face and love in your heart!

Don't allow your relationship to become complacent. Every self-help book out there says make time for each other. Have date nights—they do help.

Stand strong against the forces that try to come between you. Remember: your partner is not the enemy. You are both in the same boat, trying to achieve the same goals. It's you both, together against the world, because united you'll stand, divided you'll fall!

God Bless.

By Troy Williams

www.ingramcontent.com/pod-product-compliance
Lightning Source LLC
Chambersburg PA
CBHW020339130626
46549CB00003B/1214